THE HIP-HOP REVOLUTION

KANYE WEST

CONQUERING MUSIC AND FASHION

TOM HEAD AND
DEIRDRE HEAD

Published in 2020 by Enslow Publishing, LLC.
101 W. 23rd Street, Suite 240, New York, NY 10011

Library of Congress Cataloging-in-Publication Data

Names: Head, Tom, author. | Head, Deirdre, author.
Title: Kanye West : conquering music and fashion / Tom Head and Deirdre Head.
Description: New York : Enslow Publishing, 2020. | Series: The hip-hop revolution | Audience: 5 | Includes bibliographical references and index.
Identifiers: LCCN 2018052163 | ISBN 9781978509702 (library bound) | ISBN 9781978510234 (pbk.) | ISBN 9781978510258 (6 pack)
Subjects: LCSH: West, Kanye. | Rap musicians—United States—Biography—Juvenile literature.
Classification: LCC ML3930.W42 H42 2020 | DDC 782.421649092 [B] —dc23
LC record available at https://lccn.loc.gov/2018052163

Printed in the United States of America

To Our Readers: We have done our best to make sure all websites in this book were active and appropriate when we went to press. However, the author and the publisher have no control over and assume no liability for the material available on those websites or on any websites they may link to. Any comments or suggestions can be sent by email to customerservice@enslow.com.

CONTENTS

FROM GEORGIA TO CHINA

K anye West is a superstar. Some may even say he is one of the greatest musical artists of all time. Growing up, he always knew he wanted to be great at whatever he did.

Kanye Omari West was born on June 8, 1977, in Atlanta, Georgia. Kanye's mother, Donda, grew up in Oklahoma. Her parents didn't have much money, but they paid her for bringing home good grades. As an adult, Donda earned her PhD degree, then taught college courses for people learning English as a second language.

Kanye's father, Ray, grew up in a military family. Like Donda, Ray put a high value on education. Ray took photographs for the *Atlanta Journal-Constitution,* the city's biggest newspaper. He also belonged to a black civil rights group called the Black Panthers.

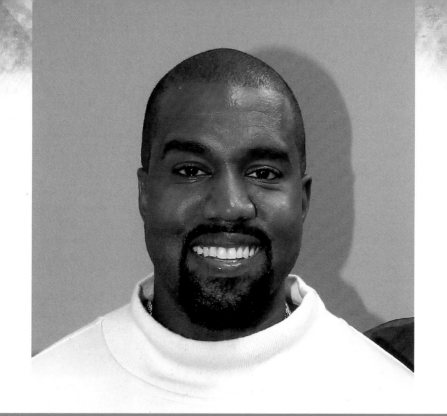

Kanye West smiles backstage at Paris Fashion Week 2016. He has become successful in music, fashion, and other industries.

Ray and Donda taught Kanye to work hard. They also taught him to believe in himself. He was their only child, and they wanted him to carry on their legacy and achieve great things.

While both of Kanye's parents were active in his life, his mother was the largest single influence. In 2007, during Kanye's early career, Donda talked about his childhood and the lessons she learned as his parent in her book *Raising Kanye*.

LIFE IN CHICAGO

Kanye's parents separated when he was still an infant. They later divorced. When Kanye was three years old, Donda took her son and moved to Chicago, where she began working as an English professor at Chicago State University. Kanye saw his father, who was still in Georgia, during the summer months.

Donda would read history books to her son instead of bedtime stories. She wanted her son to have the same love of education she had. Ray taught his son to think for himself and question everything he was told. Both parents encouraged young Kanye to love himself and

Early Talent

In preschool, the teachers noticed Kanye's drawing talent. Instead of drawing stick figures, he would draw detailed portraits of people. He was also very aware of sounds. At the park, Kanye would say that the ducks were quacking the wrong way. He was a strong-willed child with his own ideas about how the world worked.

trust his own mind. It worked. Kanye was known at a very young age to be artistic and opinionated with an all-or-nothing attitude. "I've always called Kanye a totalist," Donda said, "He's never wanted to do anything halfway."[1]

Kanye West poses with his mother, Dr. Donda West, during her 2007 book tour.

Nanjing was not very diverse, and young Kanye
felt very out of place while living there.

A YEAR IN CHINA

In 1987, Donda West was invited to teach in Nanjing,
China, for a year. This wasn't the first time she took a
teaching position outside the United States. The last
time, she had left Kanye behind. This time, she took her
ten-year-old son with her. Kanye went to school with
other children whose parents were teaching in China.

Kanye quickly found out China was very different
from the United States. He had to learn how to speak

Mandarin Chinese. He also had trouble making friends. His classmates were very curious about Kanye. Most of them had never seen a black person, and they kept trying to touch him.

Kanye learned to speak Mandarin very well, but he still felt like a stranger. When Donda realized he wasn't fitting in, she began to homeschool him. Kanye spent most of his time indoors. His days were filled with reading, drawing, and daydreaming. After their year in China, Donda and Kanye returned to the United States.

"I think being in China got me ready to be a celeb because, at that time, a lot of Chinese [people] had never seen a black person."[2]

GROWING UP IN CHICAGO

2

U pon coming back to the United States, Donda returned to her job at Chicago State University. She taught classes on a schedule that allowed her to be home when Kanye got out of school. If she couldn't be home, she would have Kanye hang out on campus.

Kanye pursued his music hobby. When he was eleven years old, he joined a dance group called the Quadro Posse. He would practice his dance moves in a mirror at home. Donda caught him practicing once and noticed his confidence.

Kanye's teachers saw him helping other contestants during talent shows. He said he was helping them because he was better than they were. He had already begun to develop a reputation for arrogance, but this reflected how focused he was. He also had wealth and fame on

Kanye performs at the South by Southwest (SXSW) music festival in 2009. His confidence and talent as a performer emerged from an early age.

his mind even at an early age. He found ways to make money off his talents. "He'd charge other kids to see him breakdance. He could spin on his head and everything," Donda said.[1]

STATE OF MIND

Kanye and his friends grew up in the 1980s. They loved listening to the music of the time. Kanye especially loved the hip-hop bands Kid 'n Play and De La Soul. Soon Kanye and his friends wanted to record their own music.

When Kanye was thirteen, he and two of his friends formed a band. They called themselves State of Mind. They rented a basement studio in Chicago for $25 an hour.[2] In a few hours, they had practiced and recorded a song. It was Kanye's first experience as a musician. He loved it.

Kanye spent his time in high school balancing his music and his grades. He started out as an honor student. But the more he got into his music, the more his grades

A Dr. Seuss Song

The song Kanye recorded with his friends was a rap song called "Green Eggs and Ham." The title came from the poem of the same name written by Dr. Seuss.

started to change. He became a B and C student. Kanye hadn't yet learned how to balance his music with other parts of his life. His interest in performing and in music was still developing.

Christopher Reid (*left*) and Christopher Martin formed Kid 'n Play in 1986 in New York City. Kanye West was a big fan of their music.

ACTING UP

Kanye West was always aware he had world-class talent. He always knew he was going to be a superstar. He always believed he was a genius. He always thought he would change the world. Today, this can make him seem eccentric. When he was a teenager, it sometimes made him hard to interact with.

Like a lot of young people, Kanye struggled with selfishness. He was full of creative ideas. Sometimes it was hard for him to realize other people had creative ideas, too. He thought he was going to get a record deal when he was thirteen. He didn't realize many other young people deserved record deals as much as he did. He didn't realize how hard it would be.

Kanye's mother noticed he had begun misbehaving at home. She told him she

"People always tell you, 'Be humble. Be humble.' When was the last time someone told you to be amazing? Be great! Be great! Be awesome! Be awesome!"[3]

Kanye West worked behind the scenes as a music producer for other artists before he hit it big as a rapper.

didn't like the person he was becoming. He promised he would do better.

When he got older, Kanye would help many young people have the same opportunities he had. He funded music education in Chicago. He also helped younger artists build their careers.

MUSIC PRODUCER

Kanye's cousin, Tony Williams, soon noticed his talent. Williams was about fourteen years older than Kanye. Williams taught Kanye how to use drum machines and sample music. Sampling music means to take a part from one song, such as the melody or some lyrics, and use it in another song. Williams also introduced Kanye to friends who worked in the music industry.

Kanye met Ernest Dion Wilson, a Chicago DJ who worked under the name No I.D. No I.D.'s mother was a good friend of Donda West. When No I.D. and Kanye first met, Kanye played "Green Eggs and Ham" for him. No I.D. was impressed by the young man's talent and took him on as a protégé. Kanye worked hard to raise money to buy studio equipment. Donda helped him get started.

Kanye also showed an early interest in fashion. His mother would give him money to buy clothes. Instead of spending it on a closet full of discount clothes, he bought a few pieces of expensive designer clothes and wore them over and over.

No I.D. gives a speech at a 2017 music industry event.
He was Kanye West's music mentor.

THE HIGH SCHOOL YEARS

Kanye was a gifted student when he was young. As he got older, his grades slipped. He was more interested in music than he was in his classes. His mother worried he might not graduate.

Kanye receives an honorary PhD from one of his hometown colleges, the School of the Art Institute of Chicago, on May 11, 2015.

He told Donda that he wanted to quit school because he found it boring. He wanted to spend his time working on beats and music.

Despite his grades, Kanye did finish high school. His creativity also helped secure a college future. Kanye entered and won national art competitions throughout high school. Thanks to these, Kanye earned a scholarship to the American Academy of Art in Chicago.

Donda was happy because her son was going to college. She believed that a good education would help her son be successful in life.

Kanye refused to choose between completing his schoolwork and managing his music career. He wanted to become successful with both, and he worked hard to try to make that happen.

An Honor

In 2015, Kanye West received an honorary PhD from the School of the Art Institute in Chicago. Earlier that year, he told Oxford University that he would have attended the School of the Art Institute "if I could have done it again."[1]

DOWN TO BUSINESS

Kanye West started at the American Academy of Art in Chicago taking painting classes. Then he changed schools and majors. He transferred to Chicago State University for English.

A local Chicago producer named Grav noticed West's talent. West wrote some songs for Grav and was paid $8,800.[2] He spent it on art and designer clothes. When Grav decided to record his first album in 1996, he went to West for help. West worked as a producer on eight tracks. The album, *Down to Earth*, was critically acclaimed and made both Grav and West famous in the hip-hop scene.

"I try to get as close to a childlike level as possible because we were all artists back then."[3]

Because of *Down to Earth*, Kanye West became a successful producer. Word spread of his talent, and he decided to drop out of college to focus on his career. He produced work for more rising artists. Soon he was working with major artists such as Jay-Z, Beyoncé, Alicia Keys, Ludacris, and Christina Aguilera.

Kanye poses for a photograph with his friend and collaborator Jay-Z in 2004.

"[Kanye] always evolved," No I.D. explained. "[E]very day is a new day, what you did yesterday don't count . . . [T]hat's how a lot of producers don't make it in the game, they get to talking about the records they did [but] it's about what you can do with this artist today."[4]

4

BECOMING A SUPERSTAR

By 2002, West was already a successful producer. But he wanted to release music of his own. He was working on his debut album, *The College Dropout,* when something terrible happened. He broke his jaw in a bad car accident that October. It could have ended his career. Instead, it made him famous. He recorded "Through the Wire" in the hospital. He rapped the song while his jaw was still wired shut. It became the first of his many hits.

West received his first Grammy Awards in 2005. He won Best Rap Album for *The College Dropout*. He also won Best Rap Song for "Jesus Walks."

A year later, he and actor Jamie Foxx released "Gold Digger." West followed this up with "Stronger" in 2007 and "Love Lockdown" and "Heartless" in 2008. By the

Kanye displays his first three Grammy trophies backstage. They were for Best Rap Album, Best Rap Song, and Best R&B Song.

end of the decade, he had undeniably become one of the most successful musicians of his generation.

West also became a fashion icon. He made shutter shades popular, and he designed sneakers for Nike and Adidas.

LOVE AND LOSS

In 2014, West married TV reality star and entrepreneur Kim Kardashian. They have three children: North, Saint, and Chicago. In 2019, they said a fourth child was on the way.

His music and fashion designs have earned him hundreds of millions of dollars. He has released

Kanye West and his wife, Kim Kardashian West, attend a 2014 fundraising event at the Metropolitan Museum of Art.

eleven hit albums. He has collaborated with almost every major artist of his time. Beyoncé, Jay-Z, Paul McCartney, Eminem, Rihanna, Drake, Nicki Minaj, Adam Levine, and T-Pain have all recorded hits with Kanye West. He has also helped launch the careers of many younger rappers, most notably Chance the Rapper. Chance was inspired to rap because of "Through the Wire."

> "As my grandfather would say, 'Life is a performance.' I'm giving all that I have in this life."[1]

In many ways, West appears to have the perfect life. However, one of the most important people is missing from it.

West's mother, Donda, died on November 10, 2007, a day after having cosmetic surgery. West blamed himself for her death. "If I had never moved to [Los Angeles]," he told Q magazine, "she'd be alive."[2] West often talks about his beloved mother in his music. He knows that he would not have the extraordinary life he has today without her support and encouragement growing up.

KANYE'S TALENT IS RECOGNIZED

Kanye West has won twenty-one Grammy Awards, the same number as Jay-Z. So far, no rapper has won more Grammy Awards than either of them. West has also won two American Music Awards, thirty BET awards, ten *Billboard* awards, twelve MTV awards, and an NAACP Image Award.

He has also achieved success as a fashion designer. His Adidas Yeezy Boost 350 sneakers won *Footwear News'* 2015 Shoe of the Year Award. Also, his clothing lines regularly draw large crowds at fashion shows all over the world.

In February 2016, a *USA Today* article asked, "Is Kanye West the Greatest Artist of the 21st Century?"[3] Whether

Giving Back

Like many others who achieved success, West has used his fame to help others. He started a music program in Chicago to support at-risk youth. He also helped raise millions for people affected by 2005's Hurricane Katrina. Furthermore, he worked on a social program to aid the poor areas of Chicago.

Wearing the shutter shades he made popular, Kanye appears at the 2007 MTV Video Music Awards. He continues to make a splash in the worlds of music and fashion.

the answer is yes or no is a matter of opinion, and the twenty-first century is still young. But *USA Today* has never published an article asking that question about anybody else. So it seems that his childhood dreams have indeed come true. Kanye West became great at what he does.

TIMELINE

1977 Kanye West is born in Atlanta, Georgia, on June 8.

1996 West begins writing and producing for Chicago rapper Grav's *Down to Earth* album, beginning his long career as a music producer.

2002 On October 2, West is injured in a bad car accident. He records "Through the Wire" while his jaw is still wired shut. It becomes his first radio single.

2004 West releases his own debut album, *The College Dropout*.

2005 West wins his first three Grammy Awards, including Best Rap Album for *The College Dropout* and Best Rap Song for "Jesus Walks."

2007 On November 10, West's mother, Donda, dies after surgery.

2009 Hoping to learn enough to become a designer himself, West takes on an internship at the Italian fashion company Fendi.

2012 West releases his first fashion collection.

2013 West's first child with Kim Kardashian, North, is born on June 15.

2014 West marries Kim Kardashian on May 24.

2015 West begins to release designer sneakers in collaboration with Adidas.

2015 His son, Saint, is born December 5.

2018 West begins offering his own line of designer homes.

2018 His daughter, Chicago, is born January 15.

CHAPTER NOTES

CHAPTER 1. FROM GEORGIA TO CHINA

1. Mark Beaumont, *Kanye West: God and Monster* (London, UK: Omnibus Press, 2015), book preview, https://www.scribd.com/book/347337479/Kanye-West-God-Monster (accessed October 22, 2018).

2. Chris Campion, "Classic Kanye West Interview: Breakdancing in China, Self Esteem Issues and the KKK," Sabotage Times, November 28, 2013, https://sabotagetimes.com/music/kanye-west-on-breakdancing-in-china-self-esteem-issues-and-the-kkk.

CHAPTER 2. GROWING UP IN CHICAGO

1. Alexandra Sakellariou, "18 Truths About Kanye West's Childhood That Reveal Why He Is the Way He Is," TheTalko, May 24, 2018, https://www.thetalko.com/18-truths-about-kanye-wests-childhood-that-reveal-why-he-is-the-way-he-is/.

2. Karizza Sanchez, "The Most Stylish #KanyeMoments from His Mother Donda West's 2007 Book," Complex, May 10, 2015, https://www.complex.com/style/2015/05/best-style-moments-raising-kanye-donda-west-book/kanye-value-quality.

3. David Samuels, "American Mozart," *The Atlantic*, May 2012, https://www.theatlantic.com/magazine/archive/2012/05/american-mozart/308931/?single_page=true.

CHAPTER 3. MUSIC PRODUCER

1. Zach Frydenlund, "Kanye West Spoke at Oxford University Earlier Today," Complex, March 2, 2015, https://www.complex.com/music/2015/03/kanye-west-oxford-university-speech.

2. Mark Beaumont, *Kanye West: God and Monster* (London, UK: Omnibus Press, 2015), book preview, accessed October 26, 2018, https://books.google.com/books?isbn=178323394X.

3. Steve McQueen, "Kanye West," *Interview*, January 14, 2014, https://www.interviewmagazine.com/music/kanye-west.

4. Beaumont.

CHAPTER 4. BECOMING A SUPERSTAR

1. Steve McQueen, "Kanye West," *Interview*, January 14, 2014, https://www.interviewmagazine.com/music/kanye-west.

2. Madeline Boardman, "Kanye West Blames Himself for Mom Donda West's Death," *Us Weekly*, June 26, 2015, https://www.usmagazine.com/celebrity-news/news/kanye-west-blames-himself-for-mom-donda-wests-death-2015266/.

3. Patrick Ryan, "Is Kanye West the Greatest Artist of the 21st Century?" *USA Today*, February 9, 2016, https://www.usatoday.com/story/life/music/2016/02/09/kanye-west-new-album/79814890/.

GLOSSARY

cosmetic surgery An operation done to change parts of the body, often to improve appearances.

diverse Made up of many different races or cultures.

eccentric Having strange habits.

entrepreneur A person who makes money by starting his or her own businesses.

honorary Describes something given as a title to recognize success.

icon Someone people look up to.

Mandarin Chinese The most commonly spoken language in China.

mentor A teacher.

producer The person who is in charge of making, and sometimes providing the money for, a record.

protégé A person guided by a mentor.

sample To take a part of a song and use it for another song.

shutter shades Sunglasses that use horizontal strips of plastic instead of lenses.

FURTHER READING

BOOKS

Burlingame, Jeff. *Kanye West: Hip-Hop Mogul.* New York, NY: Speeding Star, 2014.

Cummings, Judy Dodge. *The Men of Hip-Hop.* Minneapolis, MN: Essential Library, 2018.

Klepeis, Alicia. *Kanye West: Music Industry Influencer.* Minneapolis, MN: Essential Library, 2018.

WEBSITES

Billboard: Kanye West
www.billboard.com/music/kanye-west
Check out Kanye West's chart history, as well as videos and news.

Kanye West
kanyewest.com
Visit Kanye West's official site, with links to music videos, merchandise, and more.

INDEX